Random *Acts of*
Kindness

Random *Acts of* Kindness

365 Days of Good Deeds, Inspired Ideas and Acts of Goodness

Brenda Knight and Becca Anderson

Foreword by Megan Murphy,
founder of the Kindness Rocks Project

Conari
Press

CORAL GABLES

Cover Design: Elina Diaz
Cover Photo/illustration: stock.adobe.com/Utro na more
Layout & Design: Elina Diaz

For permission requests, please contact the publisher at:
Mango Publishing Group
2850 S Douglas Road, 2nd Floor
Coral Gables, FL 33134 USA
info@mango.bz

For special orders, quantity sales, course adoptions and corporate sales, please email the publisher at sales@mango.bz. For trade and wholesale sales, please contact Ingram Publisher Services at customer.service@ingramcontent.com or +1.800.509.4887.

Random Acts of Kindness: 365 Days of Good Deeds, Inspired Ideas and Acts of Goodness

Library of Congress Cataloging-in-Publication number: 2020946329
ISBN: (print) 978-1-64250-479-8
BISAC category code: SEL021000, SELF-HELP / Motivational & Inspirational

Printed in the United States of America

Table of Contents

Foreword:
Kindness Really Does Rock

Kindness is "love made visible," and the world has never needed it more. My path to contributing to a kinder world was the beach on Cape Cod. I decided to turn off the negativity of the morning news and take daily morning walks instead. I was at a turning point in my life, after leaving the busy and frenetic life of a retailer. What was coming next for me? I was open, albeit nervously so. The morning walks made an immediate difference in my quality of life, and I decided to paint uplifting messages on rocks and leave them where somebody who might need some positivity would see them. To my great surprise, the response was almost immediate. My painted pebbles were making an impact. And so it grew from one Kindness Rock to many across the globe. These rocks have helped grieving parents, cancer patients, adults dealing with anxiety and depression, kids struggling with a scary world, and so many people who both give and receive inspiration.

I have always loved the Random Acts of Kindness movement, and my favorite aspect of it is that these acts of goodness are often completely anonymous and done with no expectation of getting anything in return. These acts can be large and small, from paying for coffee for the exhausted single mom behind you at Starbucks, to volunteering at the local church soup kitchen, to painting a loving message on a rock and leaving it for someone who really needs it. Random Acts of Kindness actively make the world a more loving, and less painful place. What we learn from being a good in the world is that through helping others, we can find healing within ourselves.

Join the kindness revolution!

Megan Murphy
Founder of The Kindness Rocks Foundation

Introduction: Living from the Heart

We don't care what anyone else says. These are awful times. Anxiety and despair swirl around in our minds like discarded newspapers with headlines that tell us to remain on continual alert, indefinitely. Our souls are leaking. We are in a recession, and we are receding. We are not moving toward anything. We are receding away. Away from what terrifies us. Away from disease and illness, from random acts of violence and human rights abuse, from poverty and homelessness. We are both clutching each other and moving away at the same time.

In a time when so many people feel powerless and invisible, when there are so many miserable things that happen to so many wonderful people, this little book you hold is more needed than ever.

While there are moments when we must stomp our feet in indignation and make room for the expression of our outrage, we must also create space in your life for the expression of gratitude, because it is possible to surpass the suffering in the world by adding to the joy. Once you begin to perform and acknowledge random acts of kindness, you can no longer believe that what you do does not matter.

Think about the quarantined Italians who sang and danced together from their balconies during the first few months of the pandemic, holding signs bearing comforting words such as, "Come on guys, everything is going to be all right." Or think about the people in Spain, Ireland, Portugal, and France who coordinated times to applaud healthcare workers who were saving lives on the front lines. Consider the volunteers in Iran who turned shuttered mosques into makeshift spaces to sew face masks and prepare food packages for those in need. Turn your attention to the two young New York City residents who created a network of over 1,300 volunteers in just seventy-two hours in order to deliver food and medicine to elderly people in New York and New Jersey. And think about the artists and writers who offered free virtual concerts and readings to take our minds off of our worries.

What has sustained your soul? What has inspired you to hold on when all else was pulling you over a cliff? You are, we all are, the culmination of an infinite number of improbable gifts from myriad nameless sources.

And you do make a difference.

For this book, we have thought about the incredibly rich variety of ways that kindness manifests itself in the world and the effects such manifestations can have. We turned to the inspirational words of the many writers and spiritual leaders who have championed kindness in their lives and used their quotes to focus in on its wealth of nuances. We've included stories that show how that particular aspect of kindness is played out within the context of an individual's life and a meditation focal point for each week.

As the pages unfolded, we began to see that the practice of kindness has two dimensions: one is vertical, in which we deepen our connection to ourselves; the other is horizontal, in which we reach out to connect to others. Together, they create a sphere, the symbol of wholeness. Both are limitless, for there is no end to how deep or how wide you can go. But you can't have one without the other, for to serve others is to bring your wholeness—including your woundedness and your shadow—to the wholeness in others and in life.

It is our fervent hope that these experiences will assist us all to better see and respond to the opportunities we are given to bring more kindness into our lives—and into those of all with whom we share this fragile earthly home.

Brenda Knight and Becca Anderson
Editors at Conari Press

January: Start with You

"I've decided to try to be a better person... But not right away, of course... Maybe a few days from now."

—Sally to Charlie Brown in a Peanuts cartoon

So many of us say we're "trying"—trying to be more considerate of others, to take time for ourselves, to find the time to make a difference in the world—but "try" as we might, we never really get around to it. That's because *saying* we're trying can be a great escape from *doing*. We want to excuse ourselves for not doing, *and* we may want to avoid looking at the real reasons that have kept us from following through.

Week 1: Resolve to Be a Force for Good in the World

"Do or do not. There is no try."

—Yoda, a Jedi Master, in *The Empire Strikes Back*

Most of us carry around an image of ourselves as we would like to be—more generous, patient, and reliable. But what we want to be means nothing until we stop intending and start acting.

Give up trying. Next time you hear yourself saying, "I'm trying," take a moment to look at what is standing in your way of doing this thing you say you want to do. Is it that you are motivated by guilt—thinking that you "should" be doing it rather than being propelled by any sense that you want to take that action? Is it that you don't really feel like being kind because you are too angry at the world? Do you perhaps feel pressured by others, rather than motivated from your own inner desires? Or is it that you are afraid that doing it will make you too vulnerable, or that you will fail? If you find yourself "trying," stop and search instead for a puppeteer behind the curtain. Once you stop talking yourself out of taking a risk or making a difficult decision, life will open up for you and so will your mind.

Start now. Knowing who you are and figuring out ways to empower others are both important in order to have meaningful relationships with others. Think about the things that motivate and inspire you. What lifts you up—what fills you with hope and happiness? Then, think about how *you* can inspire others. Keeping your new mission as a "day lifter" in mind, make a list of short-term goals you would like to achieve by the end of this week. This task will put you on the road to kindness.

It's Never Too Late

At work a few weeks ago, I sat in on a presentation from a local nonprofit that helps underprivileged kids. The man giving the talk was someone I had gone to high school with, and, at that time, he was the most cynical guy I had ever met. Afterward, he came over to me with a big smile on his face and said, "Bet you never imagined I'd end up here." I found out that he had been heavy into drugs, was jailed countless times, and had finally ended up in a maximum-security prison for seven years. "I was the original angry man, mad at anything and everything." Then, in prison, something changed his life. Another man's kindness enabled him to clear away all the debris he had accumulated through living.

We are all born with the capacity for great kindness—it is deeply woven into the very texture of our souls. Is there a person in your life who, with a little kindness from you, can find that capacity in herself? Is it you who needs to believe more in your own innate goodness?

This week, think about what may be stopping you from being kind to others.

Week 2: Have a Mission and Live by It

"To the good I am good;
to the non-good I am also
good, for Life is goodness.
To the faithful I am
faithful; to the unfaithful I
am also faithful, for Life is
faithfulness... The person
of calling accepts them all
as his or her children."

—Tao Te Ching

What is your life purpose? If you have discovered your life's purpose, take a moment to give thanks. If you are still searching, know that the answer is there—hovering beside you, waiting for the moment when you are touched in the deepest part of your soul.

Make kindness a calling. All of us will hear the call if we listen carefully—it is the sound of our hearts pushing us to love one another, to treat each other with love and respect, to act with generosity and compassion. And each of us must find our own way of responding.

What are some ways that you can be more generous this week?

Week 3: Rewire Your Brain to Be More Positive

"People deal too much with the negative, with what is wrong. Why not try and see positive things, to just touch those things and make them bloom?"

—Thich Nhat Hanh

Not every day is filled with good things. Each of us has had dreams that for one reason or another, we do not achieve. And we may have made choices that perhaps were not the best. We endure difficult passages: illnesses, money troubles, work woes, relationship issues, the loss of a loved one, and countless others.

In order to be kind to ourselves, as well as to others, we need to learn to see our problems in their real context—to open our eyes and hearts wide enough to drink in all the beauty and joy that is always around us, no matter our tribulations.

Don't just go through it, *grow* through it. Every morning this week, even as life tries to get you down, state the intention of your day by thinking about all the good things that are going to happen. Also think good thoughts for your friends and loved ones, especially those going through difficulty.

Be kind to yourself, too. Make a commitment to refrain from negative self-talk. Dawna Markova, author of *I Will Not Die an Unlived Life,* reminds us, "Self-compassion is key to a life well-lived."

This week, write some of your weekly intentions, and as you go about your day, try keeping your mind and heart open so that you will see the benedictions of the world around you and the beauty you are capable of. Allow yourself to think good thoughts. And remember that the attitude you bring to each situation will make all the difference. All it takes is a little shift.

Week 4: Slow Down

"If you live for love, you spread kindness and compassion everywhere you go. When you stop believing in your heart, you are but a sterile vessel wandering in the wilderness."

—Francis Hegmeyer

There is a lot of hustle and bustle in this world, and it's easy to miss the simple joys of life if you are always in a hurry. Alter your perspective a bit and take your time. When grocery shopping, instead of rushing through your list, walk down every aisle, notice all the colorful fruits and vegetables, and enjoy the errand.

Here is when you know you are going too fast: when you forget to be nice.

The Eye Opener

I was living in Chicago and going through what was a particularly cold winter as far as both my personal life and the outside temperature. One evening, I was walking home from a bar where I had been drinking alone, feeling sorry for myself, when I saw a homeless man standing over an exhaust grate in front of a department store. He was wearing a filthy sport coat and approaching everyone who passed by for money. I was too immersed in my own troubles to deal with him, so I crossed the street. As I went by, I looked over and saw a businessman come out of the store and pull a ski parka out of a bag and hand it to the homeless man. For a moment, both the man and I were frozen in time as the businessman turned and walked away. Then the man looked across the street at me. He shook his head slowly, and I knew he was crying. It was the last time I have ever been able to disappear into my own sorrow.

What are some ways you could slow down this week?

Week 5: Make Time for What Matters

"There is a love like a small lamp, which goes out when the oil is consumed; or like a stream, which dries up when it doesn't rain. But there is a love that is like a mighty spring gushing up out of the earth; it keeps flowing forever and is inexhaustible."

—Isaac of Nineveh

It often takes some kind of trauma—the death of a loved one, divorce, a life-threatening illness—to wake us up to what matters. After all, no one on his or her deathbed ever regretted not spending more time at the office. Fortunately, we don't have to be facing a personal tragedy to make our relationships our number one priority. No project, no deadline, no clean kitchen is as important as the quality of your relationship with the person sitting across from you at the breakfast table, as the child who needs your attention right this second, as the mother who is alone in the nursing home.

Remembering what's important gives us the graciousness to take the time, make the phone call, send the card, and to not say the bitter retort on the tip of our tongue. When we remember what's important, we generate more loving-kindness in our lives.

What matters in your life—and what can you do this week to make time for it?

February: Don't Forget Those Closest to You

"Life is short, and we have never too much time for gladdening the hearts of those who are traveling the dark journey with us. Oh, be swift to love, make haste to be kind."

—Henri Frederick Amiel

How is it that we can go through our lives being kind and considerate to all those people around us whom we barely know, but snap or curse at, ridicule, or mistreat those we love the most? One reason is because of our vulnerability in love. When we love someone, they can hurt us so much more than others because with them our deepest wounds are exposed. It's easy to be kind when nothing is at risk.

By consciously exercising your ability to react with greater compassion and understanding with your significant other and children, you will fill your heart to overflowing and all the world will benefit.

Week 6: Look Up and Reconnect

"If I hazard a guess as to the most endemic, prevalent anxiety among human beings—including fear of death, abandonment, loneliness—nothing is more prevalent than the fear of one another."

—R.D. Laing

Unplug and make memories. Spend more time with those you love! Instead of sequestering yourselves in separate rooms watching television, playing video games, or browsing the Internet, call all family members into the same room and do something together: play a board game, watch a movie, or have everyone contribute to making dinner.

Forego using technological devices this week. Texting your friend, watching your favorite show, checking your email—all can wait! Put down your smartphone and make eye contact with your family, person to person.

Pass on the Wisdom of Grandmothers to Children Today

Rich, my beloved, was raised by his grandmother, whom he called "GM." She had been the wife of the head of their village and clan in Southern China until the Japanese Occupation, when war devastated the community at the cost of many lives. She felt very *fook sing* (lucky) to have made it to America with her only son, and they rebuilt their lives from scratch. She ran a Chinese laundry which I have no doubt was the finest in all of Flushing, Queens, or even New York. While working and taking care of her grandchildren, she told stories of the homeland, including the hardest times of having to eat insects during drought and war, famine, and pestilence. She relayed all this with no bitterness, only a sense of great good fortune in getting to live in the land of plenty in the US. Day by day, story by story, she instilled values of excellence—gratitude, hard work, keeping a positive attitude no matter what—in her children and grandchildren. When Rich and his younger brother Jimmy went to public school in Queens, they made lots of friends in that melting pot metropolis, including a young boy who was really tall for his age and came from a family that had a hard time putting enough food on the table. One day, he stopped by her house with Rich and Jimmy. It took GM about two seconds to assess the situation, and she told them to bring him by every day. She always made extra for their new fast-growing buddy. Having faced severe hunger during the war, GM was not going to let anybody in her circle go hungry. Every day, in ways large or small, she showed her family how to do the right thing—stand on the bus so others can sit, be polite even if others are rude and, above all, "Take care of your clan."

Week 7: Listening Is an Act of Love

"When one's problems are unsolvable and all one's best efforts are frustrated, it is lifesaving to listen to other people's problems."
—Suzanne Massif

Deep listening is an act of kindness not only to the other person but also to ourselves. It takes us out of our self-focus to offer empathy to another and at the same time reminds us we are not alone in our suffering. When we listen well, we are able to offer solace, companionship, and support and at the same time remember that we are really a part of a much larger community.

Just listen. Quite often, people are not looking for advice— they truly just want to be heard. Be quiet. Let the person who is talking know that you are actively listening by making eye contact; focus on the sound of their voice to avoid becoming distracted by your own thoughts or external sounds, such as a car horn or other nearby conversations.

This week, take the opportunity to truly listen to someone, if only for a brief time. Is a parent, sibling, spouse, or friend having a difficult time? Help lift their spirits by letting them experience that loving feeling. Lean forward and listen closely. Listening is one of the greatest gifts you can give anyone.

Week 8: Shower the People You Love with Love

"Charity is the bone shared with the dog when you are just as hungry as the dog."
—Jack London

Be extra nice to someone this week. Offer to help your roommate or significant other with one of their chores or do them entirely by yourself without anyone knowing. They will appreciate coming home to a vacuumed house or dinner already on the table.

Helping a Friend in Need

There was a time in my life when everything was working so smoothly that I found myself sitting at home one Saturday with all my work done and all my household chores completed: dishes washed, laundry folded and put away, house dusted, grocery shopping completed, and that delicious feeling of having nothing to do. Then I thought about a friend from work who was a single mother of two small children and never seemed to have the time for anything. I jumped into my car, drove over to her house, walked in, and said, "Put me to work." At first, she didn't really believe it, but we ended up having a great time, cleaning like mad, taking time out to feed and play with the kids, and then diving back into the chores.

Don't wait for Mother's Day or Father's Day. Celebrate your mother this week; she gave you the gift of life, and this is a sweet acknowledgement of her labor. Make your father feel special and loved.

Remember Your Parents

Like a lot of people, I've had some difficult times with my parents, especially my dad. He was like a piece of granite—harder than anything and completely immovable without a bulldozer. Growing up meant either doing things his way or paying the price. I guess part of the price was a teenage rebellion; I am still thankful I survived. I left home on my eighteenth birthday and cut myself off from my parents as completely as I could. I think it was really necessary for me to figure out who I was. It hurt my mom a lot but she kept after me. Eventually, she and I worked things out but my dad wasn't going to budge, and I sure didn't feel like bending over backward to accommodate him.

We went on like that for years. Then, when I was thirty-five, my dad died of a heart attack.

I was completely unprepared for how strongly it affected me. I hadn't talked to him for seventeen years but when I got the letter from Mom, I cried uncontrollably for hours. I guess inside I had always thought there would be time. Now he's gone, and "later" never came. The worst part is that I know I am as much to blame as he was.

It's so easy to be angry at our parents for all the ways they have failed us. And while it is important to understand and properly tend and protect the wounds we received, it is equally important to be able to accept our parents for who they are—faults and all. We need to love them for all the good things they provided us with and for all the difficult times they had to work through. And perhaps someday we may even come to appreciate that some of their failings that affected us the most dramatically are the very things that made us strong.

~~~~~~

Week 9: Celebrate Together

"Our relationships are kept moist and juicy by 'making love' all day long through conversation, presence, attention, and gentle kindness. Without dependable and meaningful connection between us, we dry up."

—Sue Patton Thoele

This week, spend time with family. Get everyone together (safely!) and spend a day at a park or at the house. Have a barbecue, play games, catch up on each other's lives, and show your gratitude for the people in your life. Leave any past disagreements at the door and see good in everyone. You love these people, and they love you. Bond over happy memories.

Make up your own holiday. Invent a special holiday to celebrate someone you love, be it your spouse, your dog, or your closest friend. On this day, make them a special dinner, take them out, and write them a letter saying how you feel about them. You can even create a fun holiday to share with your family so everyone can participate.

March: Be a Light in Dark Days

"Sometimes our light goes out but is blown again into instant flame by an encounter with another human being. Each of us owes the deepest thanks to those who have rekindled this inner light."

—Albert Schweitzer

We all have bad days. Find a way to put a smile on the face of someone who looks unhappy. Take your time, look around you, and ask yourself, "How can I help someone today?" The little things count.

Week 10: Treat People Well

"Our lives are fed by kind words and gracious behavior. We are nourished by expressions like 'Excuse me' and other such simple courtesies... Rudeness, the absence of the sacrament of consideration, is but another mark that our time-is-money society is lacking in spirituality, if not also in its enjoyment of life."

—Ed Hays

I once heard about a good deeder buying lottery tickets, adding a sweet little note, and placing them onto a car door where they could not be missed. Can you imagine if you were the recipient of this delightful act and won the big Scratch Off for a cool million or so?

This week, be more thoughtful. If you notice someone with droopy posture or a frown, why not walk up to them and say, "Good morning"? Sometimes people want to talk more than they let on, and your interest will show them you care. If you notice a friend or coworker struggling, bring them a bagel or coffee to take their mind off of their challenges, if only for a moment.

The Baseball Mitt

When I was in college, I worked part-time at a sporting goods store. There was a kid who would come by two or three times a week to visit with this baseball mitt that he wanted to buy. My manager and I would joke about him not only because he was so dedicated and persistent, but also because he had picked the best and most expensive mitt in the shop to become obsessed about.

This went on for months. The kid would come in, and you could tell he was so relieved that the mitt was still there. He would put it on, pound his fist into the pocket of the glove a couple of times, and then very carefully put it back onto the shelf and leave. Finally, one day he came in with a shoe box and a smile about eight miles wide and announced that he wanted to buy the mitt. So the manager brought the mitt over to the cash register while the kid counted out a shoe box worth of nickels, quarters, and dimes. His stash came to exactly $19.98.

The mitt cost $79.98, not including tax. My manager looked at the price tag, and sure enough the 7 was a little smudged, enough that a desperately hopeful seven-year-old could imagine it to be a 1. Then he looked at me, smiled, and very carefully recounted. "Yep, exactly $19.98." Wrapping up the mitt, he gave it to the boy.

Share your kindness randomly, aware that you may never really know the effect your action will have, and treasure each precious offering you receive.

Week 11: Be Ripsniptious!

"Mental sunshine will cause the flowers of peace, happiness, and prosperity to grow upon the face of the earth. Be a creator of mental sunshine."

—Anonymous graffiti

Simply put, "ripsniptious" (rip-snip-shuss) can be used to express something or someone that is wonderful and highly spirited. This week, you will be ripsniptious and notice all of the other ripsniptious things around you. Let this be your word of the week and let it embody you!

Spread Mental Sunshine

I worked for an insurance company for five years while I was going to school at night; it was a very difficult and stressful time of my life, made infinitely worse by the committed pettiness of the company. We lived by production quotas and the time clock; we even had to clock out and in for our breaks. The whole office of about forty people was just beaten down by the cruel regimen, except for one woman who I swear brought us all through each day.

She was the most cheerful person I ever met. Fortunately for us, her job was to drop off and pick up the files we were supposed to be churning out, so she passed by all of our desks several times a day. No matter what, she walked through that office like a radiant beam of sunshine on a heavily overcast day. I don't know how she came by such a joyful disposition, but I for one never would have made it without her.

Live Aloha. In the beautiful paradise known as the Hawaiian Islands, there is a tradition of "Living Aloha." In Hawaiian culture, *aloha* includes the concepts of kindness, bringing unity, politeness, humility, and endurance. If you live your life with simple acts of goodness every day and follow the tradition of native Hawaiian islanders, you will surely become good in the world.

Week 12: Create Glad Days

"Shall we make a new rule of life from tonight: always to try to be a little kinder than is necessary."
—Sir James M. Barrie

This week, go ahead and tell someone how thankful you are for having them in your life. A genuine compliment can boost someone's confidence, and that is a great feeling. Write a letter to an old college professor. Say thank you to a colleague. Call the restaurant manager about the great experience you had with an enthusiastic waiter.

Finding positives and accentuating them is the easiest way to turn proverbial frowns upside down and gray skies back to blue. Who are some people in your life who could use some "glad days" this week?

Week 13: Learn the Art of Letting Go

"The grudge you hold on to is like a hot coal that you intend to throw at somebody else, but you're the one who gets burned."

—Buddhaghosa, around the fifth century, BCE

After all, we are all human and we have a little baggage (or a lot)! Sometimes we hold in our feelings until they are like a dam about to overflow. Allow yourself to let go of the past so that you can proceed to live in the present without worry, fear, or resentment. We often think of forgiveness as something we do for the other person, but forgiveness is really a kindness toward ourselves. When we hold a grudge, it stands in the way of love and kindness flowing into and out of our lives. Once you relieve yourself of the burden that has been weighing you down, you can heal.

Get Rid of Grudges

My neighbor's husband left her twenty years ago, and she refuses to get over it. I can't tell you how many times I have had to hear her stories of what a complete jerk he was. The sad thing is that she is right; he was a jerk, and what he did and how he did it was mean, completely insensitive, and cruel. I know because he told me. He also told me that he tried to tell her the same thing many times, to acknowledge his wrongdoing and give her his apology, but he finally gave up because she doesn't want to hear it. She thinks it's just him trying to be forgiven, and she isn't about to forgive him. The irony is that she thinks forgiveness will "let him off the hook," but she's the one that's still hooked. He remarried and is very happy, and she has been alone and bitter for twenty years.

Is there someone you need to forgive this week? Or is it you who needs to make amends? Apologize to someone you've wronged. By admitting fault and letting them know how sorry you are to have hurt them, you are taking responsibility for your actions and proving that you care enough for them to make things right. However bad you felt over the problem, you will feel five times better after making peace.

Week 14: Friends Are Not Just for Facebook

"Friendship takes work. Finding friends, nurturing friendships, scheduling face time, it all takes a tremendous amount of work. But it's worth it. If you put

in the effort, you'll see the rewards of positive friends who will make your life extraordinary."

—Maya Angelou

Friendship is one of the most important things in the world, and it is not just a phenomenon that takes place on social media. When somebody moves, we are there to help pack and tape up boxes. When somebody is sick, we are there with homemade soup and a listening ear. There are the occasional squabbles but when trouble comes knocking, we have each other's backs all the way. It's a beautiful thing.

How can you improve your friendships this week?

Write letters and send postcards. Many people have shunned snail mail as a way to communicate. This makes letters a rare, but very inexpensive surprise. When I receive a letter, I get a rush of endorphins, because I'm holding proof that a friend thought of me. Letters are my personal therapy, my rush of endorphins, my connection to those I love, and my alone time— my regular servings of happiness.

Gather for good. Plan an outing with a group of friends that will positively impact society. Instead of just going to the movies again, gang up for the good of all. Together, plant a community garden, help clean up a schoolyard, or volunteer for a nonprofit organization.

Think about how you can create little moments of happiness for others this week. Help a friend plant her garden, buy an extra coffee for a coworker, take your kids to a movie, or wash the dishes in your office kitchen. All those little things can add up to *big* joy. Make someone happy!

April: Honor the Earth That Gives Us Life

"Remember, remember
the sacredness of things
running streams
and dwellings
the young within the nest
a hearth for sacred fire
the holy flame."
—Omaha Indian chant

We live in a wonderland of beauty and mystery. The more we hone our skills of observing, listening, and connecting to all that surrounds us, the greater and deeper the wealth of peace, joy, and beauty we will have. Take the time to feel the air on your face and to marvel at the majesty of weather. Feel yourself as part of the extraordinary nature of our world, and let it fill you with its blessing.

Week 15: Celebrate Earth Day Every Day!

"He that plants trees loves others besides himself."
—Thomas Fuller

Earth Day is celebrated annually on April 22 in over 184 countries to promote a healthy environment and peaceful planet. But we should acknowledge our connection to our home planet and all the nurturing, bounty, and beauty we receive from this big blue dot *every* day.

This week, think about ways to make every day Earth Day. Choose from action steps like these:

- Join an organized group and help clear beaches and parks of trash and recyclables.

- Petition your local government for more trees, cleaner waterways, and an end to industrial pollution.

- Use earth-friendly chemicals at home and at work.

- Recycle paper and cans, and compost green matter from the garden.

What else can you think of?

The Secret Gardener

I moved into a new house a few years back. It was the first time I had a yard of any size. There was a small lawn with about thirty rosebushes, six camellias, five rhododendrons, and numerous smaller plants, which at the time I could not even name. I was a bit overwhelmed and not doing a very good job of maintenance—especially in terms of cutting the grass.

After a few weeks, I noticed—vaguely—that something seemed different when I came home one evening. But I didn't pay too much attention. Then one day, I came home to find freshly cut grass, precisely trimmed around the edges and all around the sidewalks and driveway. I realized that someone had been weeding and pruning almost every day while I was away at work.

Finally, I caught the culprit in the act—my eighty-six-year-old neighbor, Mr. Okumoto. It's now been seven years, and he's still doing it; not only in my yard, but the one behind his house and the one on the other side of his.

Week 16: Be Water Wise

"Water is life's matter and matrix, mother and medium. There is no life without water."
—Albert Szent-Gyorgyi

We take water for granted. We sometimes leave the faucet running when we brush our teeth, overwater our gardens, wash the car too often, take baths every evening rather than a quick shower, or neglect mending that dripping tap.

Every drop of water counts. This week, make a commitment to becoming water wise:

- Take shorter showers.

Ditch the high-maintenance front lawn and choose native plants that require less or *no* water.

- Get a rain barrel.

- Give up bottled water.

Three gallons of water provide the daily drinking, washing, and cooking water of one person in the developing world... yet in the US, that flushes one toilet a single time. Three gallons of water weigh 2.5 pounds. Women in Africa and Asia carry, on average, twice this amount of water over four miles...each and every day. It puts things into perspective.

Week 17: Be a Protector of the Ocean

"There's nothing more beautiful than the way the ocean refuses to stop kissing the shoreline, no matter how many times it's sent away."

—Sarah Kay

Oceans are the lifeblood of our planet and all the creatures that live here. They cover nearly three-quarters of the earth and hold 97 percent of our planet's water. Let's celebrate our oceans, which generate most of the oxygen that we breathe, feed us, and regulate the planet's climate.

This week, look into one of these activities:

- Volunteer to clean up your local beach.

- Learn about the Ocean Cleanup and their method of cleaning up almost half of the Great Pacific Garbage Patch in just ten years at theoceancleanup.com— get involved!

- Visit surfrider.org and learn about the international nonprofit organization dedicated to the protection and enjoyment of the world's oceans and beaches through conservation, activism, research, and education.

Week 18: Save the Planet, One Tree at a Time

> ## "There must be more to life than having everything!"
> ### —Maurice Sendak

Trees hugely improve the quality of our lives. They provide shelter and food for our wildlife, clean the air, absorb carbon dioxide, and release oxygen. They mask noise, prevent soil erosion, and provide wood for fuel and buildings: all this plus the joy and wonder of such majestic and wonderful growing things.

This week, commit to one of the following activities:

- Save a tree by recycling paper. Be planet-positive and go paperless. Try paying bills online. By some estimates, if all households in the US paid their bills online and received electronic statements instead of paper, we'd save 18.5 million trees every year, 2.3 billion tons of carbon dioxide and other greenhouse gases, and 1.7 billion pounds of solid waste.

- Plant a suitable tree in your garden or neighborhood and dedicate it to someone special. Grow your own garden, even if it is just on a stoop, windowsill, or fire escape: fruits, vegetables, and herbs, oh my! Think of the recipe possibilities if your ingredients were right in your own backyard. Also, there are some indoor plants that can actually purify the air—they look great, produce oxygen, and can even absorb contaminants like formaldehyde and benzene. And if you want to be generous, go ahead and plant a fruit tree near the fence or street. Put up a little sign that says, "Help yourself!" Friends let friends forage.

- Plant flowers in abandoned lots. Brenda plants flower seeds in neglected plots of land all around the Bay Area, particularly nasturtiums, which thrive on neglect and can bloom anywhere and under any circumstances. She could give you a driving tour of San Francisco and the East Bay and show you the brightly colored patches that are the result of her Johnny Appleseed-style scattershot approach.

- Help save the rainforest by donating to the Rainforest Action Network at ran.org or supporting the Nature Conservancy's amazingly ambitious goal of planting a *billion* trees and restoring the forests of the world. Visit them at nature.org.

Tropical rainforests are the single greatest terrestrial source of the air that we breathe. Rainforests are home to over a thousand indigenous tribal groups as well as thousands of species of birds, butterflies, exotic animals— all of which are now endangered. Rainforests also affect rainfall and wind all around the world by absorbing solar energy for the circulation of our atmosphere. The trees provide buffers against wind damage and soil erosion, which then help prevent flooding along our coastlines. Tragically, rainforests are being destroyed at an alarming rate. More than an acre and a half is lost every second of every day. That's an area more than twice the size of Florida going up in smoke every year!

- Encourage community management of forests. Work with local communities and environmental NGOs to establish sustainable community forestry that benefits everyone. Get involved at treesforthefuture.org and meet your fellow tree huggers!

The Giant Oak Tree

I had just graduated from college and had gone back to the town I grew up in to visit friends. My parents had sold the family home a few years back and moved out of state, so I also took the opportunity to drive by the old house just to see it. Out in the front yard, perched in "my" giant oak tree, was a boy about ten years old. I stopped the car, went over to introduce myself, and told the boy that when I was his age, I'd practically lived in that tree. He thought that was really funny because he said his mother was always telling people that he lives in that tree.

While we were standing there talking, laughing, and feeling very good about our shared tree, a car drove up to the curb right in front of us. A middle-aged man got out of the driver's side, came around to the passenger side, and helped a very frail-looking old man out of the car. I guess we were both staring, but the old man just walked right up to the tree, patted it on the side, looked at us, and said, "I planted this tree sixty years ago when there was nothing here but fields. I still like to come visit it now and then." Then he turned around, got back into the car, and drove away. We were both so shocked we didn't say a word until after the old man had left. Then the boy just looked at me and said, "Wow."

May: Protect Our Natural Resources

"Until every individual feels personally responsible for the careful planning and preservation of natural resources, the inexorable destruction will go on."

—Eda LeShan

The universe around us is vast. When we peer out from our tiny little planet at stars and planets that are tens if not hundreds of light-years away, we are brought up short as far as our sense of human self-importance and we are reminded that we are part of something much bigger than ourselves. And in the flow of time, perhaps this is not such a bad thing, because we have been given an opportunity to redefine our destiny so that it includes things more fundamental and essential than expansion and competition. Let's not contribute to the squandering of our many natural resources in a mad rush of consumerism.

Week 19: Let's Do Something about Preserving Natural Resources and Our Planet

"Because normal human activity is worse for nature than the greatest nuclear accident in history."
—Martin Cruz Smith

This week, do something against pollution and picture how the world might change from your one tiny act. By believing in the depth and lasting strength of environmental kindness, we can find inspiration and move into action.

- **Remember that true love does not require a diamond.** We cannot discuss jewelry without acknowledging that many people pay a steep price in order to mine, produce, and export all those shiny little rocks we coyly call "a girl's best friend." There are so many ways to show your love, and no suffering should be involved—ever.

- **Avoid plastic.** Use jars. Use aluminum foil and wax paper. Reuse empty yogurt, sour cream, or cottage and cream cheese containers. Invest in reusable lunch containers like bento boxes or tiffins.

- **Spare the air.** Support our scientists by letting our elected officials know we need fossil fuel alternatives: wind power, solar power, and wave power. Choose more earth-friendly transport, which also reduces smog-causing emissions. Recycle, conserve energy, and support the work of Environmental Defense and other environmental organizations. Stop smoking.

- **Recycle your cell phone.** Cell phones and batteries are some of the largest contributors of toxic substances to our landfills. Go to epa.gov for more information on how to recycle your cell phone.

Week 20: Save and Recycle

"The greatest threat to our planet is the belief that someone else will save it."
—Robert Swan

We are born into a world that is rich with beauty. It is there for us at every moment so that we may replenish our hearts, rekindle our enthusiasm, and keep in mind how much we have to be grateful for in our lives. We must protect our planet's life systems. Saving and recycling saves the rainforest.

Here are some actions you may take this week:

- **Save the planet one paper towel at a time.** Ditch the paper towels and facial tissues. Tea towels and dishcloths work pretty much everywhere you'd use a paper towel, and you can employ newspaper for the truly gnarly messes. Shop for some pretty handkerchiefs and carry one in pocket or purse; they will easily replace tissues when you need to blow your nose and will save you money as well.

- **Make daily decisions to put less garbage into the waste stream.** Diaper with a conscience. By the time a child is potty-trained, a parent will have changed between five and eight thousand diapers; including all children in disposable diapers, this adds up to approximately 3.5 million tons of waste in US landfills each year. Use cloth diapers or a more environmentally friendly disposable alternative.

- **Don't contribute to the great Pacific garbage patch.** Nearly 90 percent of plastic bottles are not recycled; these bottles take thousands of years to decompose. If you are used to buying and toting around your green tea, juice, or iced coffee in plastic, get a cool-looking thermos instead and do DIY drinks (which, aside from being eco-friendly, will also save you big bucks off of single person sized pre-bottled beverages).

- **Be a pre-cycler.** Try to recycle all the product packaging that an item comes in, from the cardboard box to the plastic sleeve. Buy fewer but better-quality products to ensure you won't end up with a makeup drawer filled with stuff that doesn't live up to its promises. Also, check out companies like TerraCycle (terracycle.com) that offer recycling programs for things like mascara tubes and lotion bottles.

- **Be a freecycler.** Offering your surplus and finding what you need for free are both gratifying experiences, and ultimately, they alleviate a lot of stress on our precious planet. Join a Freecycle group at freecycle.org and begin to post messages about what you want and what you have to offer.

- **Recycle glass.** Every ton of glass recycled saves the equivalent of nine gallons of fuel oil needed to make glass from virgin materials.

Week 21: Reuse

"There is no such thing as 'away.' When we throw anything away, it must go somewhere."
—Annie Leonard

In addition to recycling, strive to reimagine and reuse whatever you are able to every chance you get. When wrapping presents, use old maps or even newspapers—or cut open a paper grocery bag, flip it over, and have your kids customize the paper with their artwork. You can also keep and reuse gift bags and tissue paper you were once given. This will save you money on buying gift wrap while helping to save a few more trees.

For your action steps for this week, you can:

- **Bring reusable shopping bags when heading to the store.** Whether you are grocery shopping or heading out with friends to splurge on clothes, take your own bags with you. Many stores have totes and reusable bags for a few dollars by the checkout lines that are more durable, hold more objects, and last much longer than those flimsy paper and non-biodegradable plastic bags.

- **Become a modern digger.** There is plenty of free stuff to be found in every community. Urban foraging or "dumpster diving" has become very popular in the last few decades. If you fancy learning the skills necessary for successful dumpster diving, Freegans (freegan.info) are the people to contact.

- **Hold a closet swap soirée** so you can share your surplus clothes with friends and acquaintances. This is a fun way to exchange clothes as well as other items.

- **Moving and grooving.** Green your packing efforts when it's time to relocate. Moving? Use clean sheets, pillowcases, and towels to pack breakable items like dishes and framed artwork. The soft material will help cushion your breakables, reducing or eliminating the need for bubble wrap.

- **Being a visionary.** Did you know your old specs can have a second act? Old prescription eyeglasses can be donated to a LensCrafters store. Every LensCrafters business supports OneSight, which provides glasses to millions of people around the globe. Learn more at lenscrafters.com/onesight.

Seeing the Sky

I live high in the hills, and my body is getting old. One day, I was out in my garden fussing with weeds and grew tired. I decided to lie back on the grass and rest like I used to when I was a small boy. I woke up some minutes later with a neighbor whom I had never met leaning over me, all out of breath, asking me if I was ok. He had looked out his window from two blocks up the hill and saw me lying on my back on the grass, looking, I am sure, like the victim of a stroke or heart attack, and had run all the way down the hill to check on me. It was embarrassing, but it was also so wonderfully touching. After we had it all sorted out, he let out a deep breath and lay down on the grass beside me. We both stayed there very quietly for a while, and then he said, "Thank you for deciding to take your nap out on the lawn where I could see you. The sky is such a beautiful thing, and I cannot remember the last time I really looked at it."

Week 22: Save Energy

"Solar power, wind power, the way forward is to collaborate with nature—it's the only way we are going to get to the other end of the twenty-first century."

—Bjork

The easiest way to save energy is to power down. Switch off lights when you leave a room, don't leave the faucet running if you're not actively using it, use energy-saving light bulbs, opt for blankets over turning on the heater, and choose portable fans over air conditioning. All of these will lower your utility bills and help preserve the planet. It just makes *cents* (get it?).

Here are some things you can do this week:

- **Turn off your computer at night** instead of leaving it on or in sleep mode, since this wastes energy.

- **Use a dishwasher.** This might surprise you, but washing dishes by hand uses six times as much water and twice the amount of energy as built-in dishwashers do per load.

- **Lighten the load laundry puts on our environment.** At the store, look for phosphate-free, eco-friendly laundry detergent powder. And remember that dryers are energy vampires. Clotheslines are better. Hang dry your wet laundry.

- **Try global cooling instead.** According to the folks at Environmental Defense, whenever you save energy—or use it more efficiently—you reduce the demand for gasoline, oil, coal, and natural gas. Less burning of these fossil fuels means lower emissions of carbon dioxide, the major contributor to global warming.

Week 23: Practice Conscious Eating

"Never doubt that a small group of thoughtful, committed citizens can change the world; indeed, it is the only thing that ever has."

—Margaret Mead

Think about what you eat—and what it does to the environment.

This week, consider doing the following:

- **Cut back on meat consumption**. Eating less meat is good for the environment, your health, and your wallet. Producing one pound of beef puts as much carbon dioxide into the environment as driving a typical car seventy miles! Also, the next time you consider grabbing a burger at a fast food place, remember this: over the past few decades, the rainforests have been disappearing to satisfy our hunger for cheap beef. Rainforests are a precious part of our ecosystem. Let's all do something to protect them. Over five million acres of South and Central American rainforests are cleared each year for cattle grazing. The local people don't eat this much meat—it is exported to make one-dollar hamburgers or cheap barbeque meals.

- **Support farm-to-school projects.** By teaching kids exactly where their food comes from, they will grow up to make informed grocery choices and strengthen their local economies. Start a farm-to-school project in your school district; all the know-how is at farmtoschool.org.

- **Detox your diet.** Buy grass-fed, hormone-free, organic, and free-range meat, dairy, and eggs. Many grocery stores now have organic sections with produce that doesn't contain chemical fertilizers, pesticides, or herbicides. These choices are better for you and the earth because no chemicals go into the soil or water. Also, just say no to GMO.

Go solar. Solar ovens are inexpensive and easy to use, and you'll cook for free every time you use one. Since it doesn't require electricity, fossil fuels, or propane, a solar oven is perfect for your emergency supply kit. They also pasteurize water for drinking. Go solar and really worship the sun.

Our world is a deep well of kindness from which we can draw. So walk through it with open eyes and an open heart, and it will fill you to overflowing.

June: Don't Be a Stranger

"We cannot live only for ourselves. A thousand fibers connect us with our fellow men; and among those fibers, as sympathetic threads, our actions run as causes, and they come back to us as effects."

—Herman Melville

Acknowledge other people: Such a simple thing can mean an awful lot. Be open to conversing with new people and becoming friendly with them. If you're at a bookstore and see someone holding a book you like, strike up a conversation and ask them about it. And be accepting of everyone for who they are. Embrace the beauty of humanity and our myriad differences. By opening your eyes and mind to the possibility of love and friendship, new people will flow into your life and change your perspective in miraculous ways.

Week 24: Just Say Hello

"Put your heart, mind, intellect, and soul even to your smallest acts. This is the secret of success."
—Swami Sivanada

This week, smile as you walk past someone. Maybe it's the barista handing you your much-needed double-shot latte in the morning, your neighbor planting flowers by their lawn as you go to check your mail, or a stranger walking their dog down the street. A simple, genuine smile can brighten someone's day as well as yours: so simple, so nice.

Week 25: Be of Good Cheer

"The purpose of life is a life of purpose."
—Robert Byrne

Open the doors for everyone—young, old, everyone in between—simply because it is a very, very, very nice thing to do. Holding the elevator: a simple yet kind idea. If you are inside an elevator and see someone approaching as the doors close, hold the doors open to let them in. You might make a nice connection, and the person will appreciate this gesture. Rack up those positive karma points.

Write love notes. Make a sign that reads, "Take what you need," with tear-off tabs on the bottom that say, "love," "courage," "optimism," and so on; hang it up in places you regularly pass by. Leave encouraging, inspiring, or funny notes or quotes in a library book or other random places (without littering or defacing public property; say, inscribed on a bookmark). A simple note stapled to a bulletin board, taped to a column, or written in chalk on the sidewalk may influence in wonderful ways—you'll be like a secret agent who brings happiness to others. Or write a note of gratitude to the people in your everyday life who make a difference—the mailman, a grocery clerk, or the greeter at the mall. Just by paying attention to those who can so easily go unnoticed, you can enrich each other's lives a little each day.

The Answering Machine

Who would ever think that a telephone answering machine
could change your life? I had just broken up from a long and
very painful relationship and found myself suddenly in a new
city with no friends, without anything to do or any desire to
do anything. I was like a listless blob of expended energy.
Every day I would come home from work and just stare
at the walls, sometimes crying but mostly just sitting and
wondering if this cloud would ever go away.

I had bought an answering machine—why, I don't know,
since nobody ever called me. One night, I came home and
the red light was flashing. I couldn't believe it, a phone call.
When I played it back, a wonderful male voice started to
apologize, saying he had called the wrong number, and I
burst into tears. But then he kept talking. He said my voice
on the message had sounded so sad and he just wanted to
tell me that it was ok to be sad, that being able to feel that
sadness was important. His message went on for almost
twenty minutes, just talking about how important it was to
be able to go through the pain instead of running away from
it, and how even though it probably seemed impossible now,
things would get better. He never even said his name, but
that message was, in a very important way, the beginning
of my life.

Week 26: Be a Good Samaritan

"By the accident of fortune, one may rule the world for a time, but by virtue of love and kindness, one may rule the world forever."

—Lao-Tsu

Doing a favor for someone without expecting something in return is the epitome of kindness. This week, get acquainted with the power of simple human kindness and easy acts of goodness every day. When at the grocery store, return the shopping cart or offer to help the elderly man struggling with his bags. Open doors for people. Say "Hello" with a smile. Every day and in every way choose to take the high road in your travels. The view is much more beautiful from up top!

Some other ideas:

- **Cartloads of kindness.** You'd be surprised how many people don't put their shopping carts away once they are done unloading their groceries! Walk the extra ten feet to the nearest shopping corral and roll the cart on in. Done! In addition, if you notice someone about to put their cart away and you need one, offer to take their shopping cart. These momentary connections that can happen in the frozen food aisle or parking lot are good for us; they keep us human and even help keep us together.

- **Use your common cents.** Next time the person in front of you in line at the cash register is short a few cents, give them the amount they need. If you see a car parked in a metered spot that is about to run out of time, slide in some loose change to help them avoid a parking ticket. Sometimes the driver is just a few minutes late and a ticket is almost a 100 percent guarantee to spoil someone's good day.

- **It's the thought that counts.** Leave something useful in an area where it will be most needed: an umbrella next to a public doorway or a spare bag at the grocery store for those who forgot theirs. Leave extra coupons on the shelf next to the item they are for. Practice tiny acts of kindness! Easy peasy!

- **Pay it forward.** Stop for a moment and think of something kind that someone once said to you. With gratitude for what was given, reach out and give back. It can be a simple gesture, like sending a card or calling someone who is sick and saying you care. We have all needed help now and again, and maybe somebody spent time they didn't have in order to help us out in the past. Return the favor and be that person who is prepared to walk an extra mile.

Flying High

I flew into O'Hare Airport and had a two-hour layover before my connecting flight. So I went to the first bar I could find, ordered a drink, opened my book, and proceeded to wait out the time. Somewhere around the halfway point, I pulled out my ticket to double-check the time of departure and flight number. The gate I was leaving from was almost at the opposite end of the airport, so I left what I thought was plenty of time to get there and check in. By the time I made it all the way over to the right gate, though, I was almost the last person in line to board. That's when I realized my ticket was missing.

There I was, checking every pocket, emptying the contents of my briefcase, rechecking my pockets, and all the time I had this sick feeling in my stomach that I had left the ticket on the table in the cocktail lounge at the other end of the airport. Just as I was about to go into a major panic, a man comes running up to the gate and says, "I found this ticket on a chair in the bar. When I saw what flight it was for, I figured maybe I could catch you in time." I barely had time to thank him before I was rushed onto the plane and the doors closed.

Week 27: Love and Lattes

"Kindness is more important than wisdom, and the recognition of this is the beginning of wisdom."

—Theodore Isaac Rubin

Leave a tip and a little thank-you note in the tip jar at your favorite ice cream shop. Put in little "good job" notes in the tip jar at your local café. Good work should be acknowledged, and people should know they are appreciated (and so should their boss)!

During the pandemic, many Americans have "paid it forward" by leaving thousands of dollars in tips to help restaurant staff during closures. A Houston couple left a $9,400 tip at Irma's Southwest. In Ohio, a costumer left a $2,500 tip to be split among employees after hearing their favorite bar would be forced to close down.

Sunshine on a Rainy Day

I have been going to the same bagel and coffee shop every Sunday for years. One morning in the middle of a great dreary drizzly weekend, I trudged in dripping wet with my newspaper carefully tucked under my overcoat and ordered my usual bagel with lox and cream cheese and an espresso. I was casually informed that my coffee had already been paid for. I looked around expecting to see some friend sitting somewhere, but didn't, and, when I asked, the young woman at the register just smiled and told me someone had paid for twenty coffees and I was number eight. I sat there for almost an hour, reading my paper, and watching more surprised people come in to find their morning coffee paid in advance. There we all were, furtively at first and then with big funny smiles on our faces, looking at everyone else in the restaurant trying to figure out who had done this incredible thing, but mostly just enjoying the experience as a group. It was a beautiful blast of sunshine on an otherwise overcast winter day.

Go ahead and make someone's day. Some shops have punch cards that offer a free product after a certain amount of purchases. When you reach the limit, before you cash it in to get a free item, give the card to someone in line behind you and surprise them with a free coffee, frozen yogurt, or sandwich! You can also treat someone to a meal—this is especially effective when people least expect it! Whether you are out with a friend or see a person in need on the street, take the opportunity to buy their meal without offering. Just do it.

July: Be a Good on Your Own Block

"Everyone can be great because everyone can serve."

—Martin Luther King Jr.

Many of us can readily contemplate kind acts when we think about either those closest to us—our family and friends—or those farthest away, like people starving in Somalia or dying in Bosnia. But sometimes the hardest place to keep in mind is our own neighborhood. Sometimes we don't even have a notion of what our community is. What is your sense of your neighborhood? How many streets does it encompass? Is it just the four houses around you? Do you know your neighbors? Do you know your neighborhood's needs and concerns? This month, just notice your relationship to your neighborhood.

Week 28: Look to Your Neighborhood

"So many people say they want to save the world. Just try your block, will you?"

—Rev. Cecil Williams

True generosity, with no strings attached, expecting nothing in return and without scorekeeping, is a direct expression of abundance. Make a list of small things you can do around your neighborhood to conserve energy and water, stop waste, and increase recycling. Then start doing them! Good neighbors can last a lifetime and bring a real sense of community on a daily basis.

This week:

- **Have a good neighbor policy.** Bring your neighbor's newspaper to their front door. When you go to take out your own garbage and recycling, knock on your neighbor's door and offer to take hers out, too. Offer to take care of a neighbor or friend's home, yard, or pets while they are away on vacation. Watch a neighbor's children so they can run errands or spend time with their significant other. Greet your new neighbors with a homemade housewarming gift. Make dinner for new parents the day they come home with their baby; a healthy and delicious meal with plenty for leftovers can ease parents' way home and into their new routine.

- **Be a tourist in your own town.** Go for a stroll around the city you live in. Pay attention to the little things you may have been missing, such as the architecture, the perfect picnic spot in a park, the greenery, and the people around you. Spend your money where your heart is, your own community. Support local agriculture and business by purchasing produce or baked goods from farmer's markets. Every dollar you spend locally will go a long way toward supporting your local economy *and* your next-door neighbors.

Week 29: Become a Miracle Worker

"I need a miracle every day!"
—Grateful Dead singer/ songwriter Bob Weir, writing with John Perry Barlow

What would it mean if you were to perform a miracle in someone's life today? It could be something as simple as taking the day off from work to spend time with one of your elderly neighbors who has been left alone or hiring one of the needy neighborhood kids to do some work in your garden. So many little kindnesses we can offer are truly miracles in the other person's eyes.

Consider yourself a miracle worker this week and see what you can generate:

- **Be a fixer-upper.** Volunteer to help build a house through Habitat for Humanity (habitat.org), or assist seniors near you with tasks like raking, shoveling, or doing minor home repairs. If you live next to an elderly couple or someone who is disabled, volunteer to help them around their yard with gardening or landscaping duties. It's also a senseless act of beauty! Ann Herbert, the poet artist who inspired *Random Acts of Kindness*, also implored us to add prettiness to the world. There are so many ways to do this: plant flowers, pick up trash, or paint a lovely mural for the entire neighborhood's pleasure. What beauty can you bring to the world?

- **Pick up and recycle or compost litter as you walk.** Sidewalks are meant for safe walking, not weaving through someone else's abandoned bottles and crumpled up take-out bags. Take pride in the area where you live and help contribute to keeping it clean and safe. One person helping can inspire many others to do the same. Find out if there's a local reuse center where you can donate things that are still viable for others.

Week 30: Move Mindfully Through the World

"This only is charity, to do all, all that we can."
—John Donne

Walk, bike, run, skip...and (re)discover the beauty of your own neighborhood. By not using your car, you are helping to reduce greenhouse gases while burning some calories at the same time!

Move mindfully through the world. Whether you're walking, driving, or catching the bus or train, don't be a distracted danger to yourself and others. Typing out a quick text may feel harmless, but texting requires visual, manual, and cognitive attention that you should be giving to your surroundings.

If you do have to drive, keep in mind that driving while texting or talking on the phone is very dangerous. Also, remember to slow down and let other drivers merge and go ahead of you, and allow every pedestrian to amble across the street, the slower the better. While you're at it, leave the parking spot up front for someone else that might need to park closer than you do, and turn off your car if you're going to be idling for more than thirty seconds (unless you are stuck at a red light). This will help save gas money, lessen air pollutants, and improve your car's fuel economy.

Two Flat Tires

I used to make an eighty-mile drive to visit my parents.
One forty-mile stretch of the road to their house is in the
middle of nowhere. One day, as I was driving alone along
this barren patch, I saw a family on the side of the road with
a flat tire. Normally I do not stop in such situations, but for
some reason I felt the need to do so that day. The family
was very relieved when I volunteered to drive them to a gas
station about ten miles down the road to get help. I left them
at the station because the attendant said he would take
them back to their car and drove on my way. About twelve
miles later, though, my car had a blowout. Since I couldn't
change the tire myself, I was stranded and unsure of what
to do. But in only about ten minutes, along came a car, and
it pulled over to offer help. It was the same family I had
stopped for earlier that day!

Week 31: Become a Citizen of the World

"It is good to have an end to journey toward; but it is the journey that matters, in the end."
—Ursula K. Le Guin

Technology has greatly changed the meaning of neighborhood and community. Learn to think globally. Start a conversation with someone of a different culture, religion, or political view while actively listening and responding. Becoming aware of someone else's viewpoints and personal journeys may enlighten how you think.

This week, think globally. Plan to:

- **Go forth and see the world.** Phil Cousineau, author of essential guides to making travel meaningful, including *The Art of Pilgrimage* and *The Book of Roads*, reminds us that travel is a very important tool for lasting happiness and creating memories to savor over a lifetime. If you cannot travel, look into acquiring a pen pal. Writing to someone in a foreign land— whether it be a soldier, a fellow student, or a long-lost relative—can really help you gain perspective and will do the same for the person you are writing to.

- **Learn the language of kindness.** Learn a new language or, if you are already multilingual, become more fluent in your less dominant language. Learning other languages will open you up to new people and cultures. A friend of mine recently took a volunteer vacation where he taught English to orphans and abandoned children in Liberia. He said he enjoyed every minute and wants to do this every year, as he loved working with the kids. As he told me this story, his smile was at least a mile wide! Teach the English language abroad!

Kindness Transcends All Limitations

Recently, I spent a year and a half traveling around the world on a tiny budget. When I returned, many of my friends expressed amazement that I could have done it, saying, "How could you get by in all those countries when you didn't have money or know the languages?"

Every time I was asked that question, my mind would flood with hundreds of memories of all the people I met who had so enthusiastically helped me each and every time I needed assistance: the little Japanese woman who led me eight blocks out of her way to the address I never could have found by myself; the Indian family that shared their sack of fresh fruit with me on the ship from Mombasa to Bombay; the old Thai woman who brought me buckets of ice and the most delicious soups as I sweated through a three-day fever in her small hotel; the African man who guided me up Mount Kilimanjaro and back in one day; the hundreds of people I met on trains, buses, and street corners who shared their smiles and greetings.

What was most true was how easy it was. The lack of ability to communicate verbally was no obstacle. Somehow, we always made ourselves understood.

Kindness is the universal language. It is the way we express our understanding that we are all simply fellow travelers in this world. Kindness breaks down all walls and crosses all borders. Kindness requires no words, no explanation. It is understood by all and can be practiced by all. In this way, it truly ties us together.

August: Care for the Animals

"Where is man without the beasts? If all the beasts were gone, man would die from a great loneliness of spirit."

—Chief Seattle

That animals can act with courage, love, devotion, and compassion is dramatically demonstrated in stories from around the world. Through their loyalty, bravery, commitment, and love, animals show more eloquently than any words might say that we are all sentient and conscious beings, each holding within us that little spark of the divine.

Week 32: Make Furry Friends

What separates the beast from us?
Our hands—our brains so ponderous?
What makes us feel superior?
We walk on two legs: they on four.
Abandoned, even pets go feral
Without love, we the world imperil
Through brutish greed, forests we ruin
And make sweet paradise a dune.
As animals respond to kindness
We humans need help with our blindness.
We mustn't be so quick to judge
We, too, must all be tamed by love.

Studies show pets provide both a psychological and physical boost to their owners. The unconditional love of a pet enables people to live longer and to recover more frequently from heart attacks, and it gives prisoners and troubled teens a way to reconnect with society. However, just as pets give people love and companionship, humans need to care for them and provide them with an appropriate loving home. Some seniors are ready for this commitment to dedicate time and affection toward a pet. This week, consider donating to petsfortheelderly.org to help a senior get a dog or a cat.

The Deer and the Deer Hunter

A man raised a pet deer that when young, was so tame it even liked to ride in the car with him like a dog. During the hunting season, they would pass other cars full of hunters whose startled gazes the deer would placidly return.

The same deer, when it was a bit older, once came upon a lost deer hunter in the woods. The hunter, completely disoriented, was startled by the deer's friendliness—it trotted right up to him, obviously tame. Figuring he had nothing to lose, the hunter decided to follow the deer. Sure enough, the deer led the man back to his house, where someone opened the door. The deer casually walked into the house.

The deer's human guardian gave directions to the now thoroughly abashed hunter, while the deer that had guided him to safety fell asleep on the couch.

Week 33: You Don't Have to Adopt to Make an Impact

"If you pick up a starving dog and make him prosperous, he will not bite you. This is the principal difference between dog and man."
—Mark Twain

If you are a parent of young children, you probably hear a steady chorus of requests for a pet. However, adopting an animal is a serious commitment. If your circumstances don't allow you to adopt or rescue an animal from a shelter yourself but you still want to make a difference in the life of an abandoned animal, consider volunteering at your local animal shelter as a dog walker, cat cuddler, or whatever else they need.

Fostering is also an excellent alternative.

- **Foster a four-legger.** You can find out if dog ownership is right for your family by checking out guidedogs.com and applying to raise a puppy for the blind. There are also many foster programs that give cat and dog lovers the chance to provide interim housing for displaced pets who have yet to find their forever home.

- **Provide food and shelter.** Next time you do your grocery shopping, pick up a large bag of cat or dog food to donate to a local animal shelter. Your goodwill will be repaid to you with many loving licks. You can also support keeping shelter dogs warm and cozy by buying a Kona Benellie blanket for your pup at konabenellie.com.

- **Rescue your friends from the farm.** Farm Sanctuary (farmsanctuary.org) is the nation's largest farm animal rescue and protection organization. You can support their efforts by visiting a sanctuary with your kids, as they often include quaint petting zoos with fuzzy critters!

Week 34: Protect the Wild Side

"I made connection with a pair of eyes, and thought, 'This is incredible; these eyes are penetrating me.' [...] It was a seeing-eye dog.

[...]
I couldn't get over it—the compassion and intensity and understanding in those eyes, and it was a dog."
—Al Pacino, about a theatrical performance

There are many ways to protect animals who live in the wilderness, including the following:

- **Feed an elephant.** Do you know how much an elephant needs to eat each day? At least two hundred pounds of chow! Check out elephants.com to find out how to feed a retired elephant all day long.

- **Adopt a wild animal.** Oceana's Adopt an Animal program (oceana.org) allows you to befriend—from a distance—a whale, manatee, puffin, sea turtle, or any number of beautiful sea creatures. Or at defenders.org, you can adopt an animal or two or you can become a member of Defenders of Wildlife and receive their excellent magazine with wildlife updates. With a donation to worldwildlife.org, you get an adoption certificate from World Wildlife Fund, a gift bag, and the long-distance love of a beastie! You can also get a photo of your new baby to show off to the relatives at holidays. (What grandparent could resist a three-toed sloth, smiley orca, or scaly anteater in the family, really?)

A Neighborly Gesture

I live in a nice town adjacent to Berkeley, California, that is very urban, but I have a big ol' backyard, which I *love*—it is the reason I live here. I have raccoons, a family of squirrels, and a pair of deer who seem to love the yard as much as I do. One of the older trees bears a huge amount of apples every fall, and I bag up the extra apples and take them to a place where deer congregate at the edge of the woods a few blocks away. Every time I deliver a new bag, I see lots of deer tracks, showing that my four-legged friends enjoy their apple a day. So, before you just compost the extra bounty of your garden or fruit trees, take a look around and see who else might appreciate a neighborly gesture.

Toto the Chimpanzee

Toto was a tame chimpanzee and the longtime companion of Mr. Cherry Kearton. When Cherry fell desperately ill with malaria, Toto sat up with him day and night. As Cherry grew weaker, Toto learned to bring a glass of quinine, the medicine needed to control the disease, to his friend.

While he was recovering but before he could rise from his bed, Cherry would signal Toto that he wanted to read. Toto learned to put a finger on each book on the shelf until the man said "Yes." Then the chimpanzee would pull the indicated book out of the shelf and carry it over to his patient. Sometimes when Cherry fell asleep with his boots on, Toto removed them for him.

In 1925, Cherry wrote: "It may be that some who read this book will say that friendship between a man and an ape is absurd, and that Toto being 'only an animal' cannot really have felt the feelings that I attribute to him. They would not say it if they had felt his tenderness and seen his care as I felt and saw it at that time. He was entirely lovable."

Week 35: Animals Have Rights, Too

"The question is not, 'Can they reason?' nor, 'Can they talk?' but rather, 'Can they suffer?' "

—Jeremy Bentham

Even with progressive legislation, our wildlife still faces a variety of threats. More than eight hundred species have gone extinct over the last five hundred years or so, according to the International Union for Conservation of Nature and Natural Resources' Red List of Threatened Species— generally considered to be the most comprehensive of its kind. Protect wildlife and endangered animals. Our diversity is what makes earth so special, and we must do all we can to preserve it.

This week, **join a preservation group or animal sanctuary** to help keep our habitats and animals safe.

Also: **Be fur-free and fabulous.** Don't buy fur, ivory, or other products derived from endangered animals, and avoid beauty products that have been tested on animals. Check with leapingbunny.org for a list of companies that do not test finished products, ingredients, or formulations on animals. You can also phone the Coalition for Consumer Information on Cosmetics at 1-888-546-CCIC; they'll be happy to send you a pocket-sized shopping guide to companies that manufacture with compassion.

Look in Surprising Places

One of the first things I noticed when we moved into our new home was the birds. Every morning I woke up to the beautiful sound of birds calling out their morning song. It was almost a year before I realized that their presence was really a gift from my neighbor, who had an elaborate bird feeder set up in her backyard just a few feet away from my bedroom window. She died this past year, and the people who moved in never kept up with stocking the bird feeder.

One day when I woke up, I felt surrounded by a cloud of sadness. I lay there for a while, trying to figure out what was causing it and finally realized it was because my morning symphony had flown. I turned toward my husband lying next to me, and he said, "It's the birds, they're gone." That day, we went to the store and bought a spectacular bird feeder and set it up in the backyard. Our morning friends are back now.

The things that nourish us, give us joy, and help the love in our hearts take many forms. Humans are so self-focused that it's easy to see people as the source and purpose of everything and forget that we are only a part of this miracle of creation. But truly "creature kindness" is around each and every one of us. Take a little time right now to notice and be thankful for the comfort and support you are given each day by the animals that surround you. And take care and act kindly toward all our companions on this journey.

September: Stand for Social Justice

"If you think you are too small to be effective, you have never been in bed with a mosquito."
—Betty Reese

The problems of the world are so immense that it's very easy to feel that nothing we can do will help. In fact, we can slowly but deliberately transform a tiny corner of the world.

Just remember:

We don't need to solve
the world's problems
today; we need only
take one small step in
that direction.

Week 36: Stand for Human Rights and Tolerance

"Pain can be an incubator for compassion if we keep our intention toward healing, learning, and serving."

—Sue Patton Thoele

It is so easy to become preoccupied with ourselves as lone individuals. After all, it is what our physical senses report to us. But we are not alone—we are just one of many, all struggling with the same issues, all trying to move in the same direction. We need each other to share the mysteries of life and death, to give substance to each other's joy and sorrows, to help us on our journey, and to remind us that we are all one. It is only when we can see every man, woman, and child as a precious and indispensable part of humanity that we bring the practice of kindness to its fruition.

Choose to embrace one of the following causes this week:

- **Stand against racism and police brutality.** Google the keywords "How to stand against racism" and create a plan of action.

- **Stand against bullying.** Over three million students are victims of bullying each year. If you see anyone being put down or harassed, stand up for them, or call the authorities if it's getting violent. Read more on how to help at dosomething.org. Stand up!

- **Support the LGBTQ+ community.** The TGI Justice Project (tgip.org) seeks to "create a world rooted in self-determination, freedom of expression, and gender justice." See how you can help! Also, take the pledge. Sign on up at itgetsbetter.org to support LGBTQ children and help teens live a bully-free life!

- **Help girls score!** Sports participation can be a huge boost to young girls' self-confidence, skill, determination, and inner success, all of which can carry through into their later years. The Women's Sports Foundation (womenssportsfoundation.org) encourages moms to get more involved with their daughter's sports. Get involved!

It's also important to **make it count** by passionately following local, national, and international events and politics. Get educated about the governance of your own neighborhood in addition to the national political landscape. Know what ideas you support and are against, and exercise your right to vote on Election Day.

Week 37: Stand Against the Abuse of Women and Children

"The only justification for ever looking down on somebody is to pick them up."
—The Reverend Jesse Jackson

Look at others through the eyes of compassion and open a place for understanding to grow. Empathize with the suffering they must have faced and hold open the possibility of their healing. In so doing, you bring compassion not only into their lives, but into your own. Each choice we make, small as it may seem, might be the grain that tips the balance or the thread that finally ties the knot for someone.

Here are a few things you can do this week to stand against abuse and violence.

- **Phone in for a good cause.** Donate your old cell phone to the National Coalition Against Domestic Violence (ncadv.org). This organization will donate the proceeds to programs that protect families who have suffered abuse. Or visit this web page, where you can choose which charities will be funded: recyclingforcharities.com/about.php.

- **Support homes and shelters.** Collect coupons for life's little essentials for personal care, buy the items, and then donate them. Homeless shelters and homes for abused women and children have been making a difference in people's lives for decades and have turned thousands of lives around.

- **Teach children to buddy up.** According to the Amber Alert website, a child goes missing every forty seconds in the United States and more than 700,000 children go missing annually. Teach your children, or the children in your family, how to be safe. Every child we save will make for a better future.

- **Join a task force.** Support organizations that care for children who have survived exploitation, enforced labor, abuse, and even slavery. On love146. org, fundraise for abolition, spread the word, or donate to the cause. GoodWeave (goodweave.org) also works to stop child labor, specifically in the rug industry. To help their efforts, donate to their One in a Million campaign.

Week 38: Care for Children and Families

"We were all children once. And we all share the desire for the well-being of our children, which has always been and will continue to be the most universally cherished aspiration of humankind."

—We the Children, at the World Summit for Children: Report of the Secretary-General

This week, make a greater effort to support the welfare of the children of the world.

- **Participate** in a charity, organization, or activity that promotes the welfare of children such as Save The Children, UNICEF, Global Movement for Children, Childreach International, Children's Defense Fund, and any others you may find.

- **Blanket children with love.** A donation to Project Night Night (projectnightnight.org) funds a nice tote bag with a blankie and a book by a top children's author for a homeless child. As for the Pajama Program (pajamaprogram.org), they provide pajamas and a book of bedtime stories to children who need them.

- **Support kicks for kids.** Check out shoesthatfit.org to donate a pair of brand-new shoes that fit perfectly for a young person who needs a leg up. Or buy a pair of shoes from Toms (toms.com), a one-for-one organization that donates a new pair of shoes to a child in need for every pair of Toms purchased.

- **Friend a family.** Sponsor a low-income rural family via boxproject.org. You can also help a family in need by donating diapers through the Diaper Bank Network at diaperbanknetwork.org. Help orphans in Kamba, Kenya, through World Vision (worldvision.org).

- **Be a good citizen.** The Outward Bound Youth at Risk Program (OutwardBound.org) helps many troubled teens get back on the road to growing up into good citizens. See how you can get involved!

Week 39: End Homelessness, Hunger, and Poverty

> # "Who are you really, wanderer?" and the answer you have to give is: "Maybe I am a king."
> ## —William Stafford

From growing up homeless to helping the homeless, NFL player James Jones knows it's better to give than to receive. "Being homeless made me a better man," says Jones. Precisely because he has known pain, Jones can empathize more deeply with the pain of others.

You, too, can show kindness and work to end homelessness, hunger, and poverty. Here are some actions you may choose to take this week. Choose courageously and generously, for each act of kindness ripples out into the world with pure potential.

This week:

- **Get involved** with Feeding America (feedingamerica. org), the largest hunger relief organization in the United States, or set up a recurring monthly donation at Action Against Hunger (ActionAgainstHunger. org), which feeds over seven million people each year. Alternatively, a donation to WholesomeWave. org provides fresh fruits and veggies to underserved communities.

- **Cook it forward.** If you love to cook and help people, this might be the option for you: Teach cooking classes or offer your services as a free guide to getting the healthiest groceries at the best prices via Cooking Matters, a division of Share Our Strength. CookingMatters.org pairs you up with a local group. And during the pandemic, Cooking Matters stated, "We're upping our online game with Facebook Live sessions, a Facebook group for support and tip-sharing, and posts with information about stretching food resources while staying at home." You can bake up a lot of love while showing others how to do the same.

- **Consider 360 degrees of giving.** The best kinds of gifts are the ones that keep on giving. A beautifully carved cutting board for your best friend's birthday from FeedProjects.com will not only impress your friend but help feed the hungry. Another option is to visit heifer.org to view and purchase some of the most helpful and generous gifts that can be given—gifts that don't fit in a box and that won't arrive on your friend's doorstep. Heifer International is an organization that works with communities to end hunger and poverty by providing sustainable agriculture and animals to families in need. You can "purchase" a goat, a flock of geese, or a hope basket, or you can browse the website for other options.

- **Stop world hunger with ten grains of rice a day.** Save a few dollars each month and donate it to a different charity. One great option for your donation is through freerice.com. For each correct answer in their online quizzes, they donate ten grains of rice to the World Food Program to help end world hunger. Think about how much rice will be donated if even half of the population did this!

The Power of a Tiny Act

Here's an apocryphal story we heard while writing *Random Acts of Kindness*. Is it true? It only matters that it could be. One day in Los Angeles a hot dog vendor, pressed by a personal emergency, turned to a homeless man and asked him to watch over his stand while he left to take care of his crisis. Hours passed. When the vendor returned, he paid the man for his time and thanked him for tending the stand. Years later, the homeless man came back, this time dressed in a business suit, and told the vendor that he was now a millionaire. "Because you gave me a chance," he said, "because you trusted me, I was able to believe in myself and turn my life around."

Life works in mysterious ways. People flow in and out of our lives like leaves floating down a river. We can see each arrival and departure as unconnected, random events, or we can search within them for a subtle, guiding hand and seize them as opportunities. What am I being called to do at this moment? What can I learn from this situation? It is so easy to get lost in the circular motion of our own thoughts that we forget that it is our *actions* that set everything—including our thoughts—in motion. Even the most insignificant-seeming action reverberates out into the world, setting off a continuously self-perpetuating chain reaction.

October: Stand for What You Believe In

"A man who won't die for something is not fit to live."

—Martin Luther King Jr.

While you might think Dr. King's words a little harsh or drastic, taking action to stand up for what you believe in is considered by many to be one of the most important values in life. What will make you take a stand? Find a cause you are passionate about, or maybe even have a personal connection to, and spend some time taking even the first steps toward taking action.

Week 40: Contribute to Education

"I don't know what your destiny will be, but one thing I do know: the only ones among you who will be really happy are those who have sought and found how to serve."

—Albert Schweitzer

It is estimated that more than fifteen million children don't have the resources they need to do well in school; teachers spend more than a billion dollars a year stocking their own classrooms due to a lack of funding in schools. Teaching others is hard work and can be a thankless job. Whether you are a student or have kids in school, approach a teacher this week and tell them what a great job they are doing. Offer to give them a hand through AdoptAClassroom.org by providing needed classroom materials so that students can succeed.

Here are some other things you can do this week to support education.

- **Keep kids in school.** Sign up to volunteer with the anti-dropout program Communities in Schools (communitiesinschools.org), or give a leg up to an elementary-school pupil who reads below grade level by tutoring them through Reading Partners (readingpartners.org). You may also choose to teach yoga, gardening, and more to middle schoolers through Citizen Schools (citizenschools.org).

- **Support your local public library.** Your patronage will make a difference!

- **Raise money** for Pencils of Promise (pencilsofpromise.org) or Precious Project (PreciousProject.org) to help provide educational opportunities in an impoverished country.

Week 41: Promote Health

"It is health that is real wealth and not pieces of gold and silver."
—Mahatma Gandhi

October is national Breast Cancer Awareness Month, so be sure to schedule an appointment with your doctor to have an exam. Men need to remind their doctors as well, as this is not just a women's issue. Remind your close friends to do the same and schedule appointments for the same time so you can go together and give moral support.

Be kind to those dealing with sickness. Listen to their fears, dish out lots of hugs, and help them in any way you can. This is one of the best things you can do with your life—using kindness to help another.

The Magic Dragon

Several years ago, when I was living in Chicago, I read in the newspaper about a little boy who had leukemia. Every time he was feeling discouraged or particularly sick, a package would arrive for him containing some little toy or book to cheer him up with a note saying the present was from the Magic Dragon. No one knew who it was. Eventually the boy died, and his parents thought the Magic Dragon finally would come forth and reveal him or herself. But that never happened. After hearing the story, I resolved to become a Magic Dragon whenever I could and have had many occasions.

Here are some things you can do this week to support the sick.

- **Turn pain into gold.** "A Sweet Touch of Hope" is a lovely piece of jewelry that represents a cancer survivor's journey to getting well and staying well. A portion of the proceeds goes to the Cancer Society, so the pendant is an emblem of hope for every woman.

- **Eat more chocolate.** When you purchase Lily's stevia-sweetened chocolate (lilyssweets.com), a portion of the profits goes to nonprofits that provide support to childhood cancer patients and survivors in Pennsylvania, California, and New York.

- **Donate movies and toys** to the children's ward at your local hospital. Even better, stay and watch a movie in the social room and bring doctor-approved treats!

- **Volunteer**—at a hospice, or for a crises center or suicide hotline. So many people are in need of help, guidance, and support.

Week 42: Help the Elderly

"If there is any kindness I can show, or any good thing I can do to any fellow being, let me do it now, and not deter or neglect it, as I shall not pass this way again."

—William Penn

This week, dedicate some time to our elders. Receiving extra one-on-one attention can be very rewarding for them, and you'll be surprised how interesting their life is once you start talking to them. Nine times out of ten, you will end up receiving much more than you give to these elders, who have wisdom, stories, advice, and love to offer.

- **Visit an elderly resident** who hasn't gotten a visitor lately at the local nursing home. Even better, use your flower power: go to the local discount store and pick up some small vases. Add a ribbon and some freshly picked flowers and deliver the arrangements to elders at a local community center, or anywhere you know they can use little random acts of roses.

- **Help the elderly with their devices.** Many senior citizens aren't tech-savvy, so volunteer your assistance to a senior who has a cell phone or computer and needs help using it. You can also sign up to teach older adults computer and technology skills through SeniorNet (seniornet.org).

- **Grant a wish to a senior citizen**. Volunteer for the Twilight Wish Foundation (twilightwish.org) to fulfill requests by donating items (like a home computer requested by a grandmother who wanted to email her grandkids, for one) or by contributing your time.

- **Just be thoughtful**. During the pandemic, major grocery stores around the world have created specific shopping times to lower the risk for the elderly and those most susceptible to the disease. What a great example of kindness!

At the Symphony

When I was a hospice volunteer, one of the patients I was assigned to look after was an elderly woman who loved classical music. For many years, she, her son, and her daughter had season tickets to the symphony. But she was way too ill to use them now. Her prognosis was only a few weeks left to live. I discussed the situation with the hospice team and we brainstormed on how we might get her to a concert. Perhaps we could put her in a wheelchair or even on a gurney and have her at the back of the theater. But in her condition, we realized that that would not work. Then I had an idea. I called the San Francisco Conservatory of Music, one of the leading schools in the country, and asked if they had a student who might volunteer to play something for a dying woman. A few days later, they sent over a very talented young woman, a violinist, who gave a private performance for the patient and her family. I wasn't at the apartment at the time, but from what the daughter told me the next day, it was glorious. She said that after the intimate living room recital, her mother told her, "In all my years of going to the symphony, that was the best concert I have ever attended."

Week 43: Crafting Kindness

"For those who dwell in the world and desire to embrace true virtue, it is necessary to unite themselves together by a holy and sacred friendship. By this means they encourage, assist, and conduct one another to good deeds."

—Saint Francis de Sales

By associating with people who are committed to doing good deeds, you will find it easier to do so also. If we seek out the angels in our midst, we are not only reminded of the power and rewards of compassion, we gain valuable insight into how to act in a loving manner.

Here are some weekly activities for you—and your kindness angels:

- **Knit and crochet with compassion.** The group Foster Care to Success's Red Scarf Project (fc2success. org/how-you-can-help/red-scarf-project/) is looking for knitters to donate homemade red scarves for foster children in school. Newborns in Need (newbornsinneed.org) would love clothing and bedding items for newborn, sick, needy, and premature babies, and Warming Families (warmingfamilies.webs.com) delivers donated blankets and other warm items to the homeless and displaced.

- **Get gifts that give back.** For every pair of thick and warm hand-knitted cable mittens purchased, CherryT Co. donates another pair to a child in need.

- **Blanket the world with love** by collecting quilts for donation. Project Linus (projectlinus.org) sends cozy quilts and oh-so-warm blankets to kids in shelters, hospices, hospitals, and wherever the cloaking comfort of love might be needed. Warm Up America (warmupamerica. org) works with community service organizations and the American Red Cross to distribute warm, handmade blankets to local organizations (or local chapters of a national organization).

- **Have a DYI Christmas, so start crafting now!** This holiday season, knit, sew, and quilt your way to a better world with the organizations below:

    ◊ The Mother Bear Project (motherbearproject. org) gives hand-knit and crocheted bears to children affected by HIV/AIDS in emerging nations so they know that they are loved.

    ◊ Socks for Soldiers (socksforsoldiersinc.com) knits socks for those on active duty serving in the Middle East.

    ◊ Stitching Up the World (candiawomansgroup. org/stitching/index.html) knits, crochets, and sews items to donate to chemotherapy patients, Special Olympics athletes, and others in New Hampshire.

    ◊ Threads of Love (threadsoflove.org) provides clothing, blankets, and other handmade articles for premature and sick infants. Threads of Love has chapters in the United States, Canada, and London, England.

◊   Tiny Stitches (tinystitches.org) is based in
    Gwinnett County, Georgia, and provides basic
    layettes to disadvantaged newborns in north
    Georgia. They also provide burial ensembles to
    families who lose an infant.

Week 44: Click to Give!

"Love is not getting, but giving. Not a wild dream of pleasure and a madness of desire—oh, no—love is not that! It is goodness and honor and peace and pure living—yes, love is that, and it is the best thing in the world and the thing that lives the longest."

—Henry Van Dyke

This week, it may take just a few keystrokes to make someone's life better. There are many websites that are click to give: just by clicking, you can help send food or money to countries and causes that need them. One of them is found at greatergood.com/clicktogive/ggc/home.

In any case, the needs of the many outweigh the needs of the few. Use Goodsearch at goodshop.com/search to search the Internet or answer survey questions. This for-profit company donates a portion of all advertising revenue to charity (50 percent of revenue or one cent for each search).

November: Make Time for Gratitude

"He alone is great who turns the voice of the wind into a song made sweeter by his own loving."

—Kahlil Gibran

When we begin a daily practice of recognizing the positive events that occur and the pleasant encounters we have with others, we will start being more thankful as the days pass. Perhaps it's someone who holds the door for you at the supermarket, the nice conversation you have with a stranger while at the coffee shop, or a hug with someone you love. These are the small moments, and often the ones we forget. Savor their beauty and what they tell you about humankind—that we do live among many good people.

Think thoughts of gratitude—two or three good things that happened today—and notice how calm settles through your head, at least for a moment. It activates a part of the brain that floods the body with endorphins, the body's natural feel-good hormones.

Week 45: Make Time for Gratitude Every Day

"It is one of the most beautiful compensations of life that no man can sincerely try to help another without helping himself."

—Ralph Waldo Emerson

When you say "Thank you" to someone, it signals what you appreciate and why you appreciate it. This week have an attitude of gratitude.

It is also a good idea to keep a gratitude journal to list the people or things you're grateful for today. The list may start out short, but it will grow as you notice more of the good things around you. Maybe someone gave you an old sofa, some sound advice, or a lift to the airport. Now list ten things that you yourself would like to give someone, then see how many of those things you can cross off in a week.

Other ideas to apply this week:

- **Teach your children well.** Sit down with your child and ask them to start a discussion about thankfulness. Provide a simple starting point: "Thank you for..." Then ask your child to draw a picture to go with the concept and get started writing the first of *many* thank-you notes for years to come!

- **Have a Gratitude Circle.** Instead of just another girls' night out, have friends over and state what you are grateful for in the world and each other. Take note! As you count your blessings, reflect on ways to give back to your community and to those less fortunate. Together, visit convoyofhope.org and find out what you can do to help.

Payback

I had an older neighbor who was very kind to me, a father figure really. After he died, I noticed that his yard had become completely overgrown; his widow was not physically able to do the gardening. So one morning, after I saw her leave for the day, I jumped the fence and put in a few hours of work. It was my way of paying him back for the care he had taken of me.

Be grateful and recognize the things others have done to help you. Remember the ways your life has been made easier or better through others' efforts. Be aware of and acknowledge the good things, large and small, going on around you. Post a "Thank you to all" on your Facebook page or your blog, or send individual emails to friends, family, or colleagues. Alternatively, send a handwritten thank-you note; these are noteworthy because so few of us take time to write and mail them. Being grateful shakes you out of self-absorption and helps you recognize those who've done wonderful things for you. Expressing that gratitude continues to draw those people into your sphere.

Week 46: Take Care of Our Veterans and Public Servants

"Let us be kinder to one another."
—Aldous Huxley, on his deathbed

Our servicemen and women are doing just that: *service*. And they should be thanked for it. Take a few moments to acknowledge their contribution and offer a friendly thank you. If you see a uniformed soldier or veteran in a restaurant, arrange to pay for their meal. Anonymously is perfect unless you want to thank them personally and possibly "enlist" a new friend into your life!

Let public workers know that they are doing a good job. When you see a fire truck, ambulance, school bus, or police car, go ahead and thank the workers inside for their hard work. Bake some goodies to take to your local police department, fire department, or teacher's lounge as a way of saying "Thanks!" Whether internally thought or externally voiced, this appreciation goes a long way.

There are many ways to pay them back:

- **Give an hour of your time.** Donate your listening services through the organization Give an Hour (giveanhour.org), and this is extremely helpful to families of vets. Listening can change lives for the better in a big way.

- **Contribute to an oral history project.** Our elders have much to share and life lessons from which we could all learn. The Library of Congress is gathering these by sending out volunteers to create video recordings for the Veteran's History Project. Get involved at loc.gov/vets.

- **Allow love to lift someone up.** If you have frequent flier miles you are not planning to use, give them to service members who have been injured in the line of duty and need to be flown to proper medical treatment. Check out fisherhouse.org to learn about Fisher House Foundation's Hero Miles Program.

Week 47: Share Stories

"Every human being
is your counterpart.
Every other human being
possesses and embodies
aspects of yourself: your
dreams, your sorrows,
your hope that your life
will not turn out to be a
dirty joke."

—Daphne Rose Kingma

Share stories with others, ones that have helped or influenced you—it may have a similar effect on them.

- **Read a child a story.** Introducing children to the world of books while they're young will help boost their imagination and intelligence (and will also strengthen your bond). Whether you are babysitting, reading to your own child, or volunteering at a library or hospital, this deed goes a long way. The fine folks at Books for Kids (booksforkids.org) help disadvantaged families collect libraries at home. You can make that happen, one kid and one book at a time.

- **Book 'Em.** Give a book to someone out of the blue. Consider their interests and buy them a book.

- **Pass on the pleasure of reading.** Look into volunteering for adult literacy classes or reading to the elderly at a retirement home at proliteracy. org. Drop off your old magazines at a retirement home, hospice, or any other place where the residents or patients may enjoy them; call or email in advance to make sure the recipients can handle an incoming donation.

- **Fight illiteracy one book at a time.** Get involved with Little Free Library, an organization that sets up charming, itty-bitty libraries outdoors in neighborhoods, where you can take a book at no charge or give one in return. Visit LittleFreeLibrary.org.

Week 48: Share Your Talents

"Through our willingness
to help others, we can
learn to be happy rather
than depressed."
—Gerald Jampolsky

"Sharing is something more demanding than giving."
—Mary Catherine Bateson

During the pandemic, museums, operas, observatories, and libraries around the world offered free cultural programs to those who were homebound; a fitness instructor in Spain offered free classes from his rooftop for people who were isolated in apartments and homes nearby; and Massimo Bottura, a Michelin-starred chef, created a "kitchen quarantine" series on Instagram, teaching basic recipes to food lovers who were stuck at home.

You can share your services and skills, too! Teach someone a craft or skill you have down. Sharing your talent with someone else may allow them to discover their own potential. Whether it's cooking, archery, or photography, spend some time doing what you love with another.

This week, teaching someone how to do something new will help you maintain your interest and establish a connection with people. No doubt you will learn just as much from being a teacher.

- **Make beautiful music.** If you're a musician living in New York City, Philadelphia, Washington, DC, Nashville, or Miami, you can volunteer through the nonprofit Musicians on Call (musiciansoncall.org) to deliver live, in-room performances to patients undergoing treatment or unable to leave their beds. Add a dose of joy to a healthcare facility by bringing the healing power of music to people who need it.

- **Music for the Soul.** When I was going through a very difficult time, someone called me up and played piano music for me on my answering machine. It made me feel very loved—and I never discovered who did it.

- **Be a mentor to someone.** Everyone needs help to achieve their dreams and goals in life. Mentorship is an excellent way of providing needed help, encouragement, and guidance. Look for opportunities to bond with and mentor people.

- **Teach what you know.** With an English degree, for instance, one of many things you can do is mentor a student in grammar and hopefully foster a love of reading, the benefits of which will last a lifetime. Check out the vast array of opportunities to teach and to learn at teachforamerica.org.

- **Help from behind the wheel.** Be a volunteer instructor in AARP's Smart Driver course (aarp.org/drive), which allows older drivers to brush up on their behind-the-wheel skills. Next time you want to give back, just put it in drive.

The Car Angel

I had just quit a job I hated and was determined to find a way to live that felt right. Money was very tight, and my car was dying on me—I mean really falling apart. A friend gave me the name of a guy who lived close to me and fixed cars. So I took my wreck to him and he fixed it. I mean he fixed *everything*—he worked on it for two days, charging me only sixty dollars. The parts alone had to have cost him quite a bit more than that! It was almost as though he'd read my soul: "This young lady doesn't have money, and she needs this car." He didn't know me from Adam. That car was my vehicle for getting to where I needed to go, and this total stranger made that possible when I really needed it.

Connections through Cancer

My wife was dying of cancer. There were lots of nonrandom kindnesses in our lives. People who knew us did many ordinary and extraordinary things. But what touched many of us in our community happened early in my wife's struggle. We decided to have a water filtration system installed in our house to take the impurities out of the water. The plumber we contacted installed the system, but then he wouldn't accept any payment. We found out later his father had died of cancer.

Sharing provides many opportunities to learn about ourselves and our capacity for kindness. It allows us to offer our resources to others and to be aided in return, and to see how generous, tolerant, or cooperative we might be. Sharing also is a way for us to treat the world more gently, by avoiding the mindless accumulation of material things. When we choose to share something, we stretch our souls and spare the earth—at least a little.

December: Give Pieces of Yourself

"For most of us, generosity is a quality that must be developed. We have to respect that it will grow gradually; otherwise our spirituality can become idealistic and imitative, acting out the image of generosity before it has become genuine."

—Jack Kornfield

In a world where money seems to count for everything, it can be so easy to lose track of what truly matters. Money can come and go, but nothing can touch the treasure we create in loving one another. Our true wealth is counted in the goodwill we show and the lives we touch. So live richly and dispense your thoughtfulness freely.

Week 49: Become an Anonymous Gifter

"Our first step in mind retraining is to establish peace of mind as our single goal. This means thinking of ourselves first in terms of self-fullness, not selfishness."

—John Templeton

This week, show someone you care.

- **Anonymously grant a wish on** someone's Amazon wish list. How simple is that? And how sweet is that? You can also grant someone a wish by donating a gift through Mercy Corps (gifts.mercycorps.org). It's as simple as this: Choose a gift on their website. The recipient gets a card that explains the gift and donation you made in their name, and your gift helps families in need.

- **Practice the art of regifting.** If your heart and wallet have different ideas about making monetary donations, it is time to summon your inner re-gifter. An unwanted gift could be a welcome donation to a charitable organization. For help selecting a charitable organization, visit the Better Business Bureau's Wise Giving Alliance at give.org. You can also contact the government office responsible for registering charities in your state. Many nonprofits have silent auction events as fundraisers; your white elephant may end up pulling in serious dollars as an auction item for your chosen charity.

- **Experiment with tithing.** There is a universal law of tenfold return. This means that when you give freely, your return is tenfold. Particularly in terms of money, many of us think the law of attraction doesn't apply: it does. Money is simple energy, and when you allow the energy of abundance to flow through you, then money and other resources continue to flow to you. When you stop the flow of abundance out of fear, anxiety, and worry, the flow of money stops.

Scatter Joy to Keep It

There once lived a man who decided to dedicate his life to helping others. He went about carrying out his purpose in a very quiet way, showing up to help a neighbor repair a roof or harvest a field, then returning home to tend his own small field. He was a good farmer and was thus able to grow many beautiful vegetables, which he gave away to those in need. One day, a terrible storm came and destroyed his home as well as his fields. His neighbors, grateful for all the kindness he had shown them, rebuilt his home twice as big, planted new crops in his fields, and filled his yard with fat pigs and healthy chickens. Looking over this bounty, the man determined that he had so much, he could expand his efforts to help others to the surrounding villages. Rather than hoard what he had, he spent it freely, constantly looking for ways to make people happy. Soon, his deeds were spoken of far and wide, and his name was praised throughout the land. People began to make pilgrimages to his farm because he was such a peaceful and loving person that just to be in his presence was a blessing. When he died after a long and joy-filled life, his village decided to preserve his home as a shrine so that whoever came there would be reminded of the magnificence of a life lived in service to others. In our own unique way, we can have as much impact as this mythical farmer. We don't have to harvest our neighbor's field or give away all that we possess. All it takes is a commitment to scatter joy: Just take a look around and see where it can be sown.

Week 50: Shed and Help Others Get Ahead

"Everything that is not given is lost."
—Indian proverb

Because we are mortal, every talent, skill, ability we possess, every thought and feeling we ever have, every beautiful sight we ever see, every material possession we own, will ultimately be lost—unless we share it. Unless we give what we have to others—to our spouse, to our child, to our friends and neighbors, to the strangers we encounter on our path—what we know and value will be irrevocably and utterly gone. This week, give freely of your mind and heart and spirit, so that who you are and what matters to you will never die.

- **Remember that one man's scrap is another man's treasure.** Redistributing surplus has been the driving force behind many nonprofit organizations serving local communities. Organizations like Goodwill and

Salvation Army collect goods to redistribute to those in need. Donation Town (DonationTown.org) will even come and pick up stuff you are ready to "free up" into the world. San Francisco's Creative Reuse Depot (a.k.a. Scrounger's Center for Reusable Art Parts) is another organization worth learning about at scrap-sf.org.

- **Give your old clothes a promotion.** Donate your unworn professional clothing to Dress for Success (dressforsuccess.org), which provides people who are transitioning to paid work with professional and casual wardrobes so they can embark on their new lives feeling like a million bucks! It's also a good idea to donate your old prom dress and shoes to the delightful folks at the Glass Slipper Project (glassslipperproject.org), a nonprofit organization that gives free prom dresses, shoes, and accessories to high school juniors and seniors. Generosity can be very glamorous! If you have too many shoes, donate your unused, new, and gently used footwear to soles4souls.org and you will help somebody who needs them more than you do.

Week 51: Become Immaterial

"Happiness is like jam. You can't spread even a little without getting some on yourself."

—Anonymous

Instead of giving stuff, you can give time. A great way to be a good in the world is to volunteer a few hours of your time to work in a soup kitchen and help serve those who are in need of a hot meal. This week, find a program like the Volunteer Resource Program at Glide (glide.org/serveameal). Volunteers assist with everything from serving food to bussing tables and handing out silverware and condiments. Be prepared to roll up your sleeves and make some beautiful human connections! You can also use this time to get your family involved and impart good moral values to your children. Make other people happy and feel your own special joy.

Here are other ways to give that do not involve material things:

- **Grow your hair for a good cause.** Donate to Locks of Love, a group that truly contributes to the good of others. Visit their website at locksoflove.org for more information.

- **Be a baby cuddler**. According to VolunteerGuide.org, "Baby cuddlers are needed in orphanages, neonatal hospital units, group homes, nurseries, and wherever else there are babies and young children who may not have adequate human contact early in life to begin developing social interaction skills." What could be better than helping a baby survive and thrive?

- **Save somebody's life.** If you have a driver's license, choose "yes" when you're asked to become an organ donor. Another good idea is to take a CPR class, because you never know when you might be in a position to put those lifesaving skills into practice. Visit heart.org to find out where you can take a class. Being prepared to save a life is smart and a *big* good. So is donating blood. Go to the American Red Cross website (redcrossblood.org/give.html/find-drive/) to find a location near you.

Week 52: Giving Benefits the Giver, Too!

"If we try hard to bring happiness to others, we cannot stop it from coming to us also. To get joy, we must give it, and to keep joy, we must scatter it."

—John Templeton

Practicing kindness keeps our souls supple and our hearts wide open; that way, whether rich or poor, wherever we find ourselves, we will stay tender, compassionate, and sensitive. Giving is healthy. "Altruism boosts immune function, improves our moods, and is linked not only to a higher quality of life, but a longer one," according to Stephen Post, at Stony Brook University. Those who help others also experience a "helper's high" when their bodies are flooded with feel-good endorphins and other natural biochemicals.

It's pretty basic: when we do good, we feel good. What will you do this week to practice kindness?

Spread It Around

I was flying home from a business trip at the end of what had been a long, hard day. I was tired and in no mood to be sociable, so of course I ended up sitting next to an unaccompanied five-year-old girl who was going to visit her grandparents. At first, I tried to ignore her, but when we were pulling back from the gate, she was gripping the armrests so hard I could tell she was really scared. So I tried to talk her through the takeoff, telling her everything was going to be fine, that it was like a really exciting ride at the amusement park.

Once we got airborne, she calmed down a bit, then turned to me with these big eyes and told me she had never been to an amusement park. I started laughing, she started talking, and the next thing I knew we were landing. I had sat there for almost two hours completely engaged in the kind of rambling, freewheeling conversation you can only have with kids. She insisted on introducing me to her grandparents, who were waiting to pick her up. As I left the terminal. I felt revived, like all the exhaustion of the day had just lifted off of me.

As this traveler found out, amazing and surprising things can happen when we extend ourselves to others. We think we are doing something because the *other* person is in need, yet it ends up that we ourselves are also renewed and refreshed. That's because when we extend ourselves for

another, we tap into an eternal river of
ever-present happiness just waiting to be drawn upon.

So remember, even when you are feeling drained and
without the slightest resources to reach out to another, the
very act of making a connection can bring you back to that
river to help wash away your exhaustion, cleanse the dirt
and grit of the daily grind, and fill you up once again with the
wonder of life.

Conclusion: The Levels of Generosity

"Peace is not something you wish for: it's something you make, something you do, something you are, and something you give away!"

—Robert Fulghum

"A man's true wealth is the good he does in the world."

—Mohammed

So many of us want peace of mind but do nothing to create it; we want love but do not commit loving acts. Kindness, love, compassion, and all the other affirmative values we desire in our lives don't just happen to us; they are generated by our decision to cultivate them within ourselves and then share them with others. If we nourish them, tend them with care, and freely give of them to others, then and only then will our lives be full of the positive attributes we long for.

What quality of mind do you long for in your life? What action can you take today that will help foster that quality? It doesn't have to be something big—a tiny step will do.

My grandmother was always a generous woman, but as she got older, her giving accelerated to the point that when I came to visit her one day, some men were hauling her dining room set out the door. I was upset because I didn't want to see her with nothing left. But she sat me down and told me, "Sweetheart, the key thing is timing. I have no desire to live in poverty, but I would love to time it so that on the day I die, I have nothing left."

Buddhists believe that generosity consists of three levels that we progress along as we practice. The first is tentative giving, in which we're not sure we want to do it. For example, we have an old sofa we're thinking of giving to Goodwill, but we hesitate: what if someday we need it? Finally, we decide it's ok to give it away and discover happiness and freedom in the giving of it, what the Buddhists call "the first joys of giving."

This makes it easier to give from the second level, which is sisterly or brotherly giving, an equal sharing of both energy and material goods as if to a loved one. With this type of giving, we feel no hesitation, rather a sense of "I have this, so let us all share in it." Friendship, openness, and a spirit of joy prevail.

The most developed generosity is called "royal giving," in which we take such delight in the welfare and happiness of others that we give the best of what we have, rather than just an equal part. With this kind of giving, writes Jack Kornfield, "It is as if we become a natural channel for the happiness of all around us."

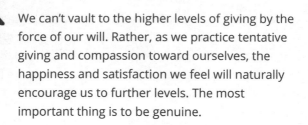

We can't vault to the higher levels of giving by the force of our will. Rather, as we practice tentative giving and compassion toward ourselves, the happiness and satisfaction we feel will naturally encourage us to further levels. The most important thing is to be genuine.

Reap the Riches of Kindness

I was graphically reminded of the true value of life one day last year when I attended two funerals on the same day. The first was for the man who owned the company I worked for. He was a very wealthy man who had built his fortune with ruthless dedication. The funeral was a very sad affair, not because he had died, but because he had left so little of himself behind. There was no outpouring of grief, nor were there any tears, just a hollow ritual of death.

The second funeral was for an old woman who had been a wonderful fixture in town for the past twenty years. She was kind of the town character, a woman without a family of her own but one who was loved by everyone. She would go to the Little League baseball games and root for whichever side was losing; she'd dress up each Halloween and walk around town, waving at all the little kids. And she always had a smile and a nice word for everyone.

Half the town turned out to say goodbye to her, and it turned into a movable party of remembrance, people remembering her antics, each sharing their own favorite stories and crying and laughing at the same time. She was a community treasure who would be sorely missed.

There is no mystery to the eternal circle of kindness. When we extend ourselves to another, we are opening our hearts to the world, and with our hearts wide open, we are poised to receive what goodness is there for us. So when you find

yourself closing down or drifting away,
reconnect to the healing flow of kindness by extending
yourself to others. It will come back a hundredfold.

Therefore, move kindly in the world, for your steps will take
you exactly where you are headed.

About the Authors

Brenda Knight began her career at HarperCollins, working with luminaries Paolo Coelho, Marianne Williamson, and Huston Smith. Knight was awarded IndieFab's Publisher of the Year in 2014 at the American Library Association. She is the author of *Wild Women and Books*, *The Grateful Table*, *Be a Good in the World*, and *Women of the Beat Generation*, which won an American Book Award. Knight is a poet, writer, and editor. She also serves as President of the Women's National Book Association, San Francisco Chapter, and is an instructor at the annual San Francisco Writers Conference, Central Coast Writers Conference and wherever she can be with fellow writers. She resides in San Francisco, CA.

Becca Anderson comes from a long line of preachers and teachers from Ohio and Kentucky. The teacher side of her family led her to become a woman's studies scholar and the author of *The Book of Awesome Women*. An avid collector of meditations, prayers and blessings, she helps run a "Gratitude and Grace Circle" that meets monthly at homes, churches and bookstores in the San Francisco Bay Area where she currently resides. Becca Anderson credits her spiritual practice with helping her recover from cancer and wants to share this with anyone who is facing difficulty in their life.

Author of *Think Happy to Stay Happy and Every Day Thankful*, Becca Anderson shares her inspirational writings and suggested acts of kindness at https://thedailyinspoblog.wordpress.com.

She also blogs about Awesome Women at https://theblogofawesomewomen.wordpress.com.